THE BOOK OF
ANGELS

THE BOOK OF
ANGELS

ALL YOUR QUESTIONS ANSWERED

BY CAROLYN TRICKEY-BAPTY

HALO PRESS

THIS BOOK IS DEDICATED TO THE LOVING MEMORY
OF HONEY, WHO WAS MY OWN "GUARDIAN ANGEL."

ANGELS CAN FLY BECAUSE THEY TAKE
THEMSELVES LIGHTLY.

—GILBERT CHESTERTON, *ORTHODOXY*

CONTENTS

CHAPTER TWO: WHAT WORK DO ANGELS DO? 33

CHAPTER THREE: WHERE AND HOW DO ANGELS LIVE? 47

CHAPTER FOUR: WHAT IS THE HIERARCHY OF ANGELS? 59

CHAPTER FIVE: WHERE DO ANGELS COME FROM? 67

CHAPTER SIX: WHAT DO THE ANGELS' NAMES MEAN? 77

CHAPTER SEVEN: WHO ARE THE MOST FAMOUS ANGELS? 81

CHAPTER EIGHT: WHAT ARE GUARDIAN ANGELS? 97

CHAPTER NINE: WHAT DO CHILDREN THINK OF ANGELS? 109

CHAPTER TEN: WHAT ARE FALLEN ANGELS? 117

NOTES

BIBLIOGRAPHY

A WORD OF THANKS

A book of this nature requires the help and support of many people, who have kindly and generously given their time to aid me in my research. I would be remiss if I did not mention their names and thank each one of "my helping angels" very much.

Thanks go to Sandy Halliday, Laurie and Barrie Chisholm, Elaine Matus, Robert Pearman, Gary Gent, Susan and Allan Lappin, Chandrani and Mohendra Wijayasinghe and Carol Jones, plus Claire Gerus and Julie Williams, my editors, all of whom were generous with their support and question-asking. To Gabriel, my sincere appreciation for overseeing the project from beginning to end. To my cousins Simon and Silvana, my brother, Allan, my sister, Lisa, and to Mom and Dad, lots of hugs and kisses for their love and generosity, and a special word of loving thanks to my wonderful husband, Eric, who gently helped and supported me throughout the writing.

I especially wish to thank Mr. Turnbull, the principal of Seba Beach School, Alberta, Canada, for his generous help in this project; Mrs. Langford, teacher at Seba Beach School, who kindly worked with the children; Janet Hunley, who gave her time to coordinate the project; Joanne Thieson-Didrikson, who started the ball rolling; the parents who allowed their children to participate; and last, but most importantly, a big hug and thank you to the children of Seba Beach. I believe the children's chapter is the gem of this book and without the support of the people at Seba Beach School, it would not have been possible.

A special thank you as well goes to Amy Gerlock, whose help and support throughout allowed me to finish the book within deadline.

WHO BELIEVES IN ANGELS?

THE MOST BEAUTIFUL THING WE CAN
EXPERIENCE IS THE MYSTERIOUS.

—ALBERT EINSTEIN

Angels. They appear in the Bible and other holy works. They star in films and TV shows. They do good deeds for humankind. But who are they? Where do they live? What do they look like?

The belief in angels goes back to the beginning of recorded time. Almost every culture on earth, whether ancient or modern, has believed that a supreme being communicated with humankind by messengers. Most often, heralds appeared to have powers unknown by humans. They seemed to be able to foretell the future. They apparently had healing powers, and most important, they offered help to individuals during times of need.

As guardians, companions and friends, angels have influenced humankind as far back as we can collectively remember. Would Mary's life have been different if the archangel Gabriel had not described to her the wondrous happenings of her pregnancy? Would Islam have been founded without Gabriel's pronouncement to the Prophet Mohammed?

Who believes in angels? Let's find out.

POPE PIUS XI
(1857-1939)

Pope Pius XI was the head of the Roman Catholic Church from 1922 to 1936. It is reputed that he spoke every morning and evening with his guardian angel. Whenever he had to deal with someone who was hostile to his ideas, he would ask his guardian angel to speak to the other person's guardian angel and sort it out between them. Apparently, the two angels would quickly come to a mutual understanding and the human meeting would proceed without discord.

SIR ERNEST HENRY SHACKLETON
(1874-1922)

Born in Ireland, this British explorer spent many years charting the Antarctic regions. He wrote that he and his companions were always aware of one more who traveled with them, providing the company with peace and safety.

HILLARY RODHAM CLINTON
(1947-   )

Hillary Rodham Clinton, wife of the 42nd U.S. President, has a gold pin that she wears on days she feels she needs special help. Her explanation? They are "angel's wings." At Christmas 1993, Hillary decorated the great Christmas tree at the White House only with angels.

PRESIDENT WILLIAM JEFFERSON CLINTON
(1946 –)

Does the President believe in angels? In his State of the Union address in February 1994, President Clinton called on Americans to honor parenthood, family and "the better angels" of their nature to combat natural and moral disasters.

POPE PIUS XII
(1876 – 1958)

Pope Pius XII wrote that everyone, no matter how humble, has guardian angels. Angels are heavenly, pure and splendid, he said, and yet they have been given to us to keep us company on our way. He explained that they have been given the task of keeping careful watch over us, so that we do not become separated from Christ. Pope Pius XII believed that not only do these angels want to protect us from dangers that waylay us, but they remain by our sides, helping us as we strive to deepen our union with God.

TAYLOR CALDWELL
(1900-1985)

Taylor Caldwell was one of the most beloved novelists of our time, and wrote such best-selling epics as *Captains and the Kings* and *Great Lion of God*. She not only believed in angels, but also acknowledged their aid in her writing. She spoke of an angel named Darios, who was always with her, helping especially when she was writing a novel. He would "appear in a burst of light, a brilliant radiance that she could not look at directly."[1] She told Jess Stearn, author of *In Search of Taylor Caldwell*, that Darios was a powerful and magnificent being and not one to be trifled with!

JOHNNY CASH
(1932-   )

Country music singer Johnny Cash has been visited twice by angels, and both times was forewarned about the death of a loved one. At the age of 12, an angel told him that his older brother, Jack, would die. Years later he was warned that his best friend, Johnny Horton, would also meet with an untimely death. In both cases, Cash felt that the knowl-

5

edge had prepared him for the death of his loved ones, making the traumatic events a little less painful.

"I can only describe [the angel] as faceless and surrounded by a brilliant, glowing light," he recalls. *"There were no wings or halo. It spoke softly, saying, 'Your brother Jack is going to die.' Then it disappeared."*[2]

BURT REYNOLDS
(1936 -   )

Upon hearing of the death of his friend, Dinah Shore, on February 24, 1994, Burt wrote the following tribute to her:

"Hollywood has lost its greatest and only angel. Dinah is what God meant when He strived to make perfection. She was the sunshine in my life and millions and millions of others.

She is the only person I ever knew who had nothing bad to say about anyone."[3]

FRANCIS SYDNEY SMYTHE
(1900-1949)

Francis Smythe climbed to within 1,000 feet of the summit of Mount Everest in 1933. During his climb, he wrote that he felt another presence close beside him.

"In [the angel's] company I could not feel lonely, neither could I come to any harm. It was always there to sustain me on my solitary climb up the snow-covered slabs. Now, as I halted and extracted some mint cake from my pocket, it was so near and so strong that instinctively I divided the mint into two halves and turned around, one half in my hand to offer it to my 'companion.'" [4]

RUSSIAN COSMONAUTS

In *A Book of Angels*, Sophy Burnham recalls this story that she read in a newspaper:

After 155 days on board the Soyuz 7 space station, three cosmonauts, Vladimir Solovyov, Oleg Atkov and Leonid Kizim, were performing medical experiments when they were blinded by a brilliant orange glow. They saw seven giant figures in the form of humans but with wings, mist-like halos, round faces and identical in appearance. They seemed to be hundreds of feet tall with a wingspan as great as a jetliner! They followed the craft for 10 minutes and then disappeared. Twelve days later the giant figures returned and three more cosmonauts saw them.

"We were truly overwhelmed," said cosmonaut Svetlana Savistskaya. "There was a great orange light and through it we could see the figures of seven angels. They were smiling as though they shared a glorious secret." [5]

WILLIAM BLAKE
(1757-1827)

This English mystic, poet and artist produced volumes of angel art. In fact, he associated all poetic genius with angels. As a young boy, he claimed to see angels in trees. And as the "scribe" of the poem *The Jerusalem,* he said that the work was dictated to him. "I am not ashamed . . . to tell you what ought to be told—that I am under the direction of messengers from heaven, daily and nightly."

SAINT PATRICK
(385-461)

Saint Patrick, the patron saint of Ireland, said his angel, Victorious, visited him every day, and that they spent many pleasant hours in conversation together.

I arise today;
in the might of the Cherubim;
in obedience of Angels;
in ministration of Archangels.

Saint Patrick

BILLY GRAHAM
(1918-)

Evangelist Billy Graham has felt so moved by the presence of angels that he decided to write a book about them. *Angels, God's Secret Agents*, became a national best-seller. In the book, he writes: "I am convinced that these heavenly beings exist and that they provide unseen aid on our behalf. I believe in angels because I have sensed their presence in my life on special occasions. Angels speak—expect them in your life."[6]

ORAL ROBERTS
(1918-)

Oral Roberts wrote about his experience with angels in his book, *Daily Blessings*:

"Angels are far more active in our lives than we realize. Once, early in my ministry while away from home on a crusade, I woke suddenly in the middle of the night, knowing my family was in trouble. I dropped to my knees and prayed, 'Lord, I'm fourteen hundred miles away from my family, so I can't help

them. Please send an angel to protect them.' Soon I became peaceful, and I knew God had answered my prayer.

"When I got home, my wife, Evelyn, told me she'd been awakened one night by someone trying to break into the house. She was terrified, but she prayed, and after a few minutes the intruder left. I asked when it happened. It was the same night the Lord had awakened me and I'd prayed for Him to send an angel to protect my family. I believe He did."[7]

TOLLER CRANSTON
(1949-)

Six-time Canadian figure skating champion, Olympic bronze medalist and a competitor on the professional North American circuit, Toller Cranston paints angelic beings with minute detail. His house in Toronto, Ontario, is filled with angel paintings and mobiles. Why? "Because they can leave gravity behind," Cranston says.[8]

JOHN BUNYAN
(1628-1688)

In *The Pilgrim's Progress*, John Bunyan described the home of the angels as the New Jerusalem, a glorious residence for the "shining ones." The angels in his book are spirits who minister to humankind, offering guidance and consolation.

MARTIN LUTHER
(1483-1546)

Martin Luther spoke of angels as "the Lord's soldiers, guardians, leaders, and protectors to preserve the creatures which He had created."

EMILY DICKINSON
(1830-1836)

As a child, poet Emily Dickinson seemed to think of angels as invisible companions. This later showed up in her work. She wrote:

"When much in the Woods as a little Girl, I was told that the Snake would bite me, that I might pick a poisonous flower, or goblins kidnap me, but I went along and met no one but Angels, who were far shyer of me than I could be of them, so I haven't that confidence in fraud which many exercise."[9]

SAINT JOAN OF ARC
(1412-1431)

Saint Joan of Arc is reputed to have seen and spoken with both the Archangels Michael and Gabriel, who gave her strength and courage to face her fate.

JOHN CALVIN
(1509-1564)

John Calvin wrote in his book, *Institutes of the Christian Religion, I*: "The angels are the dispensers and administrators of the divine beneficence toward us; they regard our safety, undertake our defense, direct our ways, and exercise a constant solicitude that no evil befall us."

LORD HUGH DOWDING
(1883-1970)

Lord Hugh Dowding was the Air Chief Marshall of the RAF, whose men fought in the Battle of Britain. In the book, *Tell No Man*, author Adela Rogers St. John related the following story:

After the war a large celebration was held to honor Lord Hugh Dowding, with the King of England, Winston Churchill and other noted celebrities in attendance. Lord Dowding told those gathered how his small number of men slept rarely and stopped flying their planes only to refuel. Men who had been hit and were dead or incapacitated were reported seen continuing to fly. Sometimes pilots in other planes would see ghostly figures at the controls. Lord Dowding said he believed that angels had flown the planes.

CHAPTER ONE

WHAT IS AN ANGEL?

ANGELS ARE SPIRITS, BUT IT IS NOT BECAUSE THEY ARE
SPIRITS THAT THEY ARE ANGELS. THEY BECOME ANGELS
WHEN THEY ARE SENT. FOR THE NAME ANGEL REFERS
TO THEIR OFFICE, NOT THEIR NATURE. YOU ASK THE
NAME OF THIS NATURE, IT IS SPIRIT; YOU ASK ITS
OFFICE, IT IS THAT OF AN ANGEL, WHICH
IS A MESSENGER.

—SAINT AUGUSTINE

WHAT IS AN ANGEL?

What do you picture when you close your eyes and think about angels? Do you picture a tall, white-robed being with golden hair and large, luminescent wings? Because angels are beings of pure energy or light, they can, and do, appear to us in many ways. There is actually no "right" or "wrong" way to see an angel.

Angels have been a part of the human experience since the beginning of recorded history. The word "angel" comes from the Greek *angelos*, meaning messenger. And much of what angels do is to communicate messages between the divine and us mortals. Sometimes they inform us about great events about to happen; other times they may warn us of impending danger. But, most important, they watch over each of us and help with the smooth running of the universe.

WHY DO PEOPLE BELIEVE IN ANGELS?

There are 375 references to angels in the Bible. And angels, in some form, are acknowledged by almost every religion on earth. A 1993 *Time* magazine/CNN poll revealed that 69 percent of Americans believe in the existence of angels.[10]

In movies such as *Rosemary's Baby*, multiple sequels of *Friday the Thirteenth*, and the books of Stephen King, evil is seen as a real and visible force. People are concerned about the rise of violent crime in neighborhoods, crimes that are shockingly vicious. A belief in angels gives people hope for a better future, and helps them feel they are not alone. People can take comfort in knowing that angels are here to help them.

DO ALL ANGELS HAVE WINGS?

People have reported seeing angels both with and without wings. When angels were first described in the Bible, they had no wings. Later, during medieval times, artists began portraying wings in their drawings of angels, apparently to show how they could appear or disappear so quickly.

Today, angels appear to people both with and without wings. Some have even appeared in modern clothing. One man reported an encounter with an angel in jeans and lace-up boots!

HOW FAST DO ANGELS MOVE?

Angels can move at incalculable speeds. Because they are beings of light, they can travel at least as fast as the speed of light. This helps explain how angels can appear and disappear so quickly. They can even materialize in one part of the world, and then another within the blink of an eye. In fact, because they travel so quickly, we rarely see them. It's only when they "slow down" that we get a glimpse of them.

HOW MANY ANGELS ARE THERE?

No one really knows how many angels there are, although some religious thinkers through the ages have tried to estimate their numbers. Theologians have argued this, particularly during the Middle Ages, and have discussed numbers in the millions.

Looking at the question today, we would include all the angels watching over each of us, as well as the plants and animals and the landscape of the earth. These alone would account for trillions of angels! And if we included those angels who watch over beings on other planets and galaxies, it would be more than we could ever imagine.

One way to look at it is to say there are likely more angels in the heavens than there are grains of sand on the beaches.

ARE ANGELS DIFFERENT COLORS, LIKE PEOPLE?

Angels appear to each of us in a very personal way. And, because they generally do not want us to be afraid of their presence, they appear in a form we will find appealing.

In most lands and cultures, many people see angels in human form. Buddhists have seen beautiful Oriental angels in flight, dressed in Chinese attire. Others have reported angels of East Indian, Native American and African background. English author C.S. Lewis said that blue and green were the colors of angels. But, as angels are beings of pure light, their actual "color" is all the shades of the rainbow. Just as a prism breaks down light into its full spectrum of color, angels are able to assume any color they choose.

CAN I BECOME AN ANGEL?

Angels were made at the time of Creation and are distinctly different from humans. We were created "in the image of God," but in a way that allows us to physically experience the earth and all the wonderful gifts that surround us. Angels can never fully experience the joy of feeling warm earth under their feet or soft rain falling on their faces.

Remember the story *The Littlest Angel?* It was about a little boy who had died and become an angel in heaven. What did this little angel miss the most? He missed the beautiful things of the earth—the rocks, the butterflies, the leather strap that had belonged to his little dog. And, although people cannot become angels, this story beautifully illustrates an important difference between angels and people. Only human beings can fully experience the physical world.

When we die, however, we may be given the opportunity to be "angel-like"—at least temporarily. There are numerous reports of people seeing recently departed loved ones hovering around their homes or in their favorite areas. Their bodies are usually luminescent, but recognizable. They often wish to comfort those left behind, relieve their grief and leave them with a sense of peace. Once they have reassured their loved ones, they apparently move on to other tasks. Real angels, of course, continue to help in our everyday lives.

HAS ANYONE EVER BECOME AN ANGEL?

There are exceptions to every rule, and history tells us of three men who did not die, but were transported directly to heaven by God and became angels. One was the prophet, Elijah, who became the most beloved angel in Jewish folklore. Another was Enoch, who, according to Gen. 5:24, "walked with God, and then he was not, for God took him." The third was Saint Francis of Assisi.

Elijah had spent many years struggling with the pagan god Baal, who had been introduced to the Israelites by Queen Jezebel. Jezebel was a tyrannical Phoenician, who had married the Israelite, King Ahab. She was devoted to Baal, and had anyone killed who did not worship him. But Elijah demonstrated the might of God and refused to bow down to Baal. In return, God recognized his good works, and took him up to heaven in a whirlwind. Here he was given a new angelic name, Sandalphon. He became a friend of the underdog and the guardian of good people in times of danger.

Enoch was a holy man of God. He was also the father of Methuselah, who lived to be 969 years old. After he was transported alive into heaven, Enoch became Metatron, one of the central angels around the throne of God. Metatron is the high priest of the heavenly temple and in charge of the guardian angels of all earth's people. We know of Enoch from the Essenes, the people of the Dead Sea Scrolls, because he was the central figure in their writings.

Saint Francis of Assisi was a kind, holy man and patron saint of the animals. He, too was taken directly to heaven, where he was transformed into an angel and given the name Rhamiel, the Angel of Mercy.

HOW BIG ARE ANGELS?

Angels apparently can be as big or as small as they wish. Geoffrey Hodson, author of several books on angels, has reported seeing angels over 80 feet tall. Others tell of angels whose bodies shone through an entire second story of their homes. One woman tells of seeing an angel when she was a little girl: *"I remember seeing a 'winged being,' garbed in a flowing white robe, completely filling the door frame. All about this presence was a luminous glowing white light."*[11]

But most frequently, angels appear to us in human form and size. Judging from their behavior when they encounter us, they do not wish to overpower or frighten us with their size. They simply wish to guide and protect us in a reassuring way.

HOW OLD ARE THEY?

While we cannot give angels an actual age, according to the Bible they have existed from the beginning of time. In Job 38:6-7, God spoke to Job about the creation of the world: "I laid the foundation of the earth. . . . while the morning stars sang together and all the angels shouted for joy." Angels existed in the Garden of Eden, and have walked with humankind ever since.

One can only imagine the amazing numbers of events the angels have witnessed, both good and bad, as the earth progressed through its many phases. And we can only guess at what the angels will watch over in the future!

DO ANGELS DIE?

Angels do not die, with the possible exception of the fallen angels (in Rev. 20:3, we are told that fallen angels will be "one day thrown in the abyss"). Jesus, reported Luke, told us angels do not die. Because angels are beings of pure energy, they have no physical body, and thus no "death" takes place. According to the Bible, their spirits live on for eternity.

CAN I TALK TO ANGELS?

Certainly! People talk to themselves, their pets and their plants, so why not to their angels? By all accounts, angels do listen, so you'd be wise to communicate your needs to them, especially during a crisis.

In the aftermath of a terrible highway accident, a woman named Marlene huddled in the wreckage of her car, trying to calm her daughter, Victoria. She remembers praying to her guardian angel for help. Rescue workers arrived almost immediately and one firefighter reached in through the smashed window to give her daughter a teddy bear, her favorite toy. Victoria stopped crying and cuddled the bear while the firefighters freed her and her mother.

Later that week, Marlene and Victoria visited the fire station to thank the firefighters for their help and for the teddy bear. But the firefighters were just a little puzzled. They never carried stuffed animals and had never given one to anyone at an accident.[12]

You can talk to your angels out loud or in your mind, whatever feels comfortable for you. Either way, they'll hear you.

CAN I SEE THEM?

Some people actually see angels, while others may hear or simply "feel" them. For example, Joan of Arc was visited by an angel who told her to lead the French army to victory. Angels can take on several forms, from cloud-like formations to balls of energy or an intense white fog.

Regardless of what shape or form they take, one thing is certain. You'll know that what you saw was an angel.

HOW DO ANGELS COMMUNICATE WITH US?

Angel communication can take many forms. It can range from a strong "knowing" to physical intervention. *For example, one woman tried to enter a building, only to be restrained by an unseen hand. When she tried again, she was physically thrown backwards. Upset, she ran away, and only later learned that there had been a criminal hiding in the building.*

At other times, the angel's voice may be clear and strong. *Clifford E. Blackman of New York was a little boy when he tried to squeeze between an oil delivery truck and a car parked on the street. He inhaled the truck's exhaust fumes and slipped under the rear tires, passing out. "The next thing I knew, I* heard a voice say, 'Push!' I pushed and opened my eyes," he re-counted. "As I did, the double rear tires of the oil truck rolled right over where my head had been." When he told his mother, she hugged him and lovingly scolded, "Never make your guardian angel work overtime like that again."[13]

Such commanding voices seem to come in times of extreme danger, or at times of anguish. The voice is not the "chatter" we hear in our head, but a different one. What is said may surprise us, but judging from people's experiences with angels, we should listen and take action if the action seems appropriate.

DO ANGELS TALK TO US IN DREAMS?

Yes, they do. We may not always remember our dreams, but our subconscious does. Sometimes we are given intriguing glimpses of the future. Sometimes warnings are given to us, as well. I was lucky enough to get some of these warnings.

A number of years ago, I was visiting Vancouver, British Columbia. My friend, Sandy, offered me her apartment while in town. One morning, at about 2:00 a.m., I had a dream. In it, I was asleep in the apartment, and woke up suddenly, thinking I smelled gas. I went into the kitchen to investigate, walking by a large mirror. When I looked into it, I saw I had no head and screamed. As I was waking up, I heard a command-

ing voice say to me over and over again, "You must call Sandy. You must call her now."

Although it was 2:00 a.m., I called Sandy at her friend's house. I told her that I felt very dizzy and uncoordinated, and Sandy urged me to get out of the apartment immediately. "I'll be right over to pick you up," she assured me. I somehow managed to crawl out of the apartment, which was filled with gas, and waited in the fresh air for her to arrive. If I had not obeyed the voice and slept until the morning, I would never have awakened. I believe an angel saved my life.

ARE CHERUBS BABY ANGELS?

The concept of child angels is solely a Western belief. Cherubs are not even shown in art until after the 1100s. Baby angels might be a carryover from other classical Roman and Greek religions which, of course, believed in Cupid. Cupid was the Roman god of love, depicted as a beautiful, naked winged boy with bow and arrows.

WHY DO CHILDREN SEE ANGELS MORE THAN ADULTS DO?

Children are, in many ways, closer to God. The veil of doubt and suspicion has not yet clouded their minds. They believe in Santa Claus, *and he exists!* They play with their invisible friends and point out angels to their parents, who are unable to see them.

Jesus said that to be as pure and simple as a child is what allows people to enter into heaven. At the Seder meal at Passover, it is the youngest child who asks the questions of the adults. Until children are taught to disbelieve their senses and only to see through adult eyes, they behold a world that is much different from ours!

CAN ANGELS SEE EVERYTHING?

Angels can see everything we do, and hear everything we say. This is possible only because their love for us is unconditional. They do not judge what we do or why we do it. They may try to prod us along a certain path, but will not stand in our way, whatever choices we make.

Some find it a little disconcerting that angels can witness all the public and private moments of our lives. But many religions teach that all our good and bad thoughts and deeds are recorded and brought before God on the Day of Judgment. Perhaps it's to our advantage that angels witness our every move. They can help us get back on track, if we lose our way, and encourage us along a path of goodness.

SOME ANGELS IN THE BIBLE SOUND VERY FRIGHTENING. WHY IS THIS?

Angels, as the messengers of God, perform His desires, and the God of the Israelites could be very forbidding. A visit from the heavenly forces often singled out a person as being special before God, which could lead to suffering and sometimes martyrdom.

The Israelites believed that angels were proud members of heaven, fighting on God's side to overcome evil and the enemies of Israel. In their dealings with humankind, angels could be harsh and judgmental. Angels of the Lord sometimes destroyed towns and armies and sent entire nations into slavery.

Old Testament scriptures serve as a reminder that we should never forget the power of angels. In the New Testament, angels were portrayed as less frightening. In fact, Gabriel's first words to Mary tell her not to be afraid, that he has come to give her wonderful news.

WHAT LANGUAGE(S) DO ANGELS SPEAK?

Angels can understand and converse in every language we know on earth, and probably beyond. Rabbinic lore concluded that angels speak Hebrew. But according to Saint Paul in one of his letters to the church at Corinth, angels have their own language.

In his book, *The Kingdom of the Gods,* Geoffrey Hodson tells us that angels "speak" in color. They communicate telepathically with one another, and while doing so, create waves of different colors around them. Perhaps because of this, we associate color with certain experiences. Why do we wrap baby girls in pink blankets and baby boys in blue? Why are we "green with envy"? Why do we "sing the blues"? Maybe we're learning how to talk like the angels!

ARE ANGELS ALL-KNOWING?

While angels might be able to see everything, we have been told that they do not know everything. The Bible says that only God is all-knowing. He alone understands why He tested Abraham by asking him to sacrifice his son Isaac, why Jesus suffered and died, and why the religion of Islam was founded. His angels follow His will, and by doing so, come closer to understanding the divine mind.

Like us, angels are constantly evolving into new and different forms, always expanding their knowledge. By acting as messengers between God and humans, they not only act as servants, but also as willing students.

WHY DO ANGELS WEAR HALOS?

Halos sometimes appear in artistic representations of angels. Perhaps those artists had encountered angels as luminescent light beings and couldn't quite come up with a way of painting them properly. Halos evolved to represent the golden light that observers had seen shining from the faces of angels. They are simply part of the light, or aura, which surrounds the angelic "body."

JESUS IS OFTEN DEPICTED IN ART AS HAVING A HALO. DOES THIS MEAN HE IS AN ANGEL?

Jesus is called the King of Angels and may command legions of the heavenly host, but he is not an angel. The halo which artists later painted around the head of Jesus was an attempt to capture the heavenly light that witnesses reported emanating from him.

CHAPTER TWO

WHAT WORK DO ANGELS DO?

THE ANGELS ALL WERE SINGING OUT OF TUNE,
AND HOARSE WITH HAVING LITTLE ELSE TO DO,
EXCEPTING TO WIND UP THE SUN AND MOON,
OR CURB A RUNAWAY OR TWO.

—LORD BYRON, *THE VISION OF JUDGMENT*

ARE THERE "BOSS" AND "WORKER" ANGELS?

There are many different levels of angels, which we might consider "boss" and "worker" levels. Later we will talk about the hierarchy of angels, but for now let's look at the work angels do here on earth.

There is a level of angels we refer to as our guardian or companion angels. Metatron is the supreme angel in charge of that group (see Chapter Seven, *Who are the most famous angels?*) All the guardian angels on earth can seek the guidance of Metatron in times of uncertainty.

From angels for animals to angels of healing, there is always another angel or archangel who can be turned to for advice.

ARE THERE ANGELS FOR EACH DAY OF THE WEEK?

The Essenes, who wrote the Dead Sea Scrolls, started and ended their days acknowledging the angels who helped them the most. These included the Angels of Sun, Air, Work, Joy, Peace, among others.

But others have also put together a table of angels and archangels who rule over the seven days of the week:

DAY	ARCHANGEL	ANGEL
Monday	Gabriel	Gabriel
Tuesday	Chimyl	Zamiel
Wednesday	Michael	Raphael
Thursday	Tzaphiel	Sachiel
Friday	Haniel	Anael
Saturday	Tzaphiel	Cassiel
Sunday	Raphael	Michael[14]

Apparently, some of these angels are expected to do double duty! There are also angels who watch over every hour of every day, which you can learn more about in Gustav Davidson's *A Dictionary of Angels*.

WHO ARE THE ANGELS OF THE ZODIAC?

The angels of the zodiac are also aligned with the angels who watch over the months of the year. They are as follows:

ANGEL	MONTH	SIGN
Malahidael	March	Aries (Ram)
Asmodel	April	Taurus (Bull)
Ambriel	May	Gemini (Twins)
Muriel	June	Cancer (Crab)
Verchiel	July	Leo (Lion)
Hamaliel	August	Virgo (Virgin)
Zuriel or Uriel	September	Libra (Scales)

ANGEL	MONTH	SIGN
Barbiel	October	Scorpio (Scorpion)
Advachiel	November	Sagittarius (Archer)
Haniel	December	Capricorn (Goat)
Gabriel	January	Aquarius (Water-Carrier)
Barchiel	February	Pisces (Fish)[15]

Again, Gustav Davidson's *A Dictionary of Angels* is an invaluable guide to find out more about the angel of a particular month or sign.

CAN ANGELS HEAL PEOPLE?

Angels do not heal people. And angels are unable to assist anyone unless the individual wishes it.

However, numerous incidents have been recorded where healing has occurred after or during an angel's visit. Tobit, a kind and holy Jew of Biblical times, was blinded by an eerie mishap. He prayed for his release from his suffering and finally God sent Raphael, the Angel of Healing, to help Tobit and restore his sight. Indeed, Raphael's name means "God has healed," and he seems to appear frequently on medical missions.

Timothy Wyllie, who co-authored Ask Your Angels, *tells in the book how he collapsed from pneumonia in 1973. He had a near-death experience where, he says, he saw his guardian angels, who gave him a choice of living or dying. He chose life.*

Upon regaining consciousness, Timothy discovered he was completely well.[16]

Angels can be willing messengers of healing. However, it is we who must ask for help.

DO ANGELS TAKE CARE OF PLANTS AND TREES?

Angels themselves do not take care of the plant kingdom, but they do oversee the nature spirits in charge of this area. The angels hold the key to the "blueprint" of how plants are formed; the nature spirits simply build from the plans. Discussing the nature spirits is best left for another book, as every culture on earth has fairy tales and stories of their "little people." However, although these spirits are not angels, they are under the protection of the angelic realm.

For those who would like to learn more about nature spirits, look up books on the Findhorn and Perelandra gardens.

DO ANIMALS HAVE ANGELS?

The theologian, Hermas, of the early church, taught that angels oversaw all affairs concerning animals. Behemiel is the Angel over Tame Beasts, Arariel is the Angel over Fish and Thegri is the Angel over Wild Beasts. In the bird king-dom, Arael is the Angel over Birds. The Dove is the only creature named who has its own angel—Alphun.

Many people believe that animals can see into other di-mensions. Have you ever had an eerie feeling when your pet dog or cat has stared fixedly at *nothing*?

In Sophy Burnham's book, Angel Letters, *one lady wrote of her dying mother, who believed strongly that there were still a number of things left to do in her life. The mother was visited in the night by four angelic beings who comforted her and gave her the strength to live for a few more weeks. How did she know there were angels there? Partly because her golden retriever, Danny, saw them as well. He nosed one out of the way so that he could lie down on his favorite spot to sleep!* [17]

CAN ANGELS PERFORM MIRACLES?

Angels can only perform miracles when guided by God's will. It's interesting that, while there is an Angel of Healing, there is no Angel of Miracles.

DO ANGELS WATCH OVER COUNTRIES AND CITIES?

Countries, states, provinces and cities all have guardian angels to watch over them. These angels are also known as Archons, or "rulers." They help to guide the mission of that area. The United States, for example, gives shelter to the homeless and needy of other nations; Canada is known for its health and welfare benefits. Each guardian sets out to guide the collective peoples of the nation or the city, leading to the betterment of the community as a whole.

According to Jewish literature, Michael is the guardian of the State of Israel, Dobiel of Persia, Samael of Rome and Rahab of Egypt. There are no named angels that I'm aware of for New York, but one would have to think there might be a horde of angels hovering over Los Angeles!

ARE ANGELS EVER INVOLVED IN WAR?

Angels can be involved in both human and angelic warfare. There are several instances in the Old Testament when the Angel of Death slaughtered thousands of armed men camped for the night.

In Christian legends, Lucifer fought to overturn the divine regime in a war that darkened the heavens. The archangel Michael defeated Lucifer and cast him into the inferno, along with about a third of the heavenly host who had joined Lucifer. In Revelation, angels under their captain, Michael, will do the bidding of their Lord Jesus battling the forces of darkness.

Perhaps the story of the Angel of Mons is the most famous account of "battlefield angels":

Shortly after World War I broke out, an angel appeared on the battlefront. During a retreat from a German assault near Mons, Belgium, both British and French soldiers reported seeing an angel in the field between their armies. The British thought they saw Saint George; the French thought they saw the archangel Michael. What made the tale more than possible hysteria was that stories from the Germans later corroborated the event. The German soldiers found themselves powerless to advance on the retreating army, and their horses turned and fled. They later said they saw thousands of troops in the Allied position, when in reality there were only two regiments.[18]

War is not a pleasant task for angels. But history tells us that they continue to fight for the best in humankind and for our ultimate redemption.

CAN ANGELS CONTROL THE WEATHER AND THE STARS?

Angels control the wind, the seas, rivers and springs and the intensity of the sun. Biblical scholar Clement of Alexandria believed that angels moved the stars, and Origen, an early Church father, declared that angels controlled the four elements. There are angels governing the four seasons, and each of these has two or three angels serving directly beneath him. There are also angels of the clouds and of the rain. Each planet in our solar system has its own guardian, seven of which are named:

Chief of the Planets: Rahatiel
Sun: Raphael
Venus: Aniel
Mercury: Michael
Moon: Gabriel
Saturn: Kafziel
Jupiter: Zadkiel
Mars: Samael[19]

Four archangels rule the four directions: Michael, the East; Raphael, the West; Gabriel, the North; and Uriel, the South.

SOMETIMES ANGELS SEEM TO HELP INTERPRET HOLY WRITINGS. IS THIS TRUE?

Certainly, this task seems to be one that angels take on with much enthusiasm. Angels helped make the Holy Writ clearer to Daniel and to Zechariah in the Old Testament, and aided John in his understanding while he was writing books that would become part of the New Testament.

Angels were also a big help in interpreting the books they gave to Joseph Smith, who founded the Mormon faith. And Muslims credit angels with helping to write and interpret the Koran, the holy book of Islam. Again, as their duty of messengers of God, angels bring people knowledge to help them evolve and strengthen their faith.

DO ANGELS EVER PUNISH US?

God has been known to send His angels to dole out punishment to humankind. The cherubim were assigned watch posts at the gateway to the Garden of Eden to keep Adam and Eve from returning to paradise; angels were sent to destroy the sinful cities of Sodom and Gomorrah. And we know from Saint Paul that God may discipline us for our own good. There are even angels and archangels of punishment. The angels of punishment are as follows:

Kushiel ("rigid one of God")
Lahatiel ("flaming one of God")
Shoftiel ("judge of God")
Makatiel ("plague of God")
Hutriel ("rod of God")
Pusiel ("fire of God")
Rogziel ("wrath of God")

These angels are ruled by the archangels of punishment, who preside over the death of mortals, animals and children, and over destruction:

Kezef (Angel of Wrath and Destruction)
Af (Angel of Anger and the Death of Mortals)
Hemah (Angel over the Death of Domestic Animals)
Mashhit (Angel over the Death of Children)
Meshabber (Angel over the Death of Animals)[20]

DO ANGELS HELP WITH THE PROCREATION OF CHILDREN?

Children seem to have a very special place in the hearts of our heavenly helpers. Biblical scholar Tertullian, along with Christian theologians Clement of Alexandria and

Origen, believed that the procreation of children was impossible without the added assistance of angels.

Amulet angels were invoked at childbirth to prevent demons from carrying the soul away. Childbearing mothers would call upon one or more of the 70 amulet angels to protect her and the newborn child throughout its life. Heading the list were Michael, Gabriel and Raphael, followed by a multitude of other lesser known angels.

ARE ANGELS GHOSTS?

Angels are not ghosts. Ghosts are the souls of human beings who have died and have chosen to stay close to the earthly plane. Sometimes they simply wish to give comfort or protect those loved ones they have left behind (as did Patrick Swayze's character in the movie, *Ghost*); sometimes their deaths are so traumatic, they have difficultly accepting that they are dead. For awhile, they remain in a state of limbo, between one world and the other.

It is important that the souls of those who have died move on to their next experiences. Their purpose is not to stay around the earthly plane to help us. It is the angels' "job" to watch over their earthly charges.

CAN ANGELS WRITE?

While there is no proof that angels have ever written an earthly best-seller, angels are said to have their own celestial alphabets, which are variations of the Hebrew alphabet. Who knows what masterpieces some may have written for the pleasure of the angelic realm!

Here are some letters from one celestial alphabet (read right-to-left):

Daleth	Gimel	Beth	Aleph
Cheth	Zaïn	Vau	He
Lamed	Caph	Iod	Theth
Aïn	Samech	Nun	Mem
Res	Kuff	Zade	Pe
		Tau[21]	Schin

45

CHAPTER THREE

WHERE AND HOW DO ANGELS LIVE?

HE . . . RODE SUBLIME
UPON THE SERAPH-WINGS OF ECSTASY
THE SECRETS OF THE ABYSS TO SPY;
HE PASS'D THE FLAMING BOUNDS OF PLACE AND TIME
THE LIVING THRONE, THE SAPPHIRE-BLAZE,
WHERE ANGELS TREMBLE WHILE THEY GAZE.

—THOMAS GRAY

ARE THERE DIFFERENT HEAVENS WHERE ANGELS LIVE?

According to ancient Hebrew texts and some medieval Christian thought, there are seven heavens—which is where we no doubt get our expression, "I'm in seventh heaven!" The higher the heaven, the closer one is to the ecstasy of being near the divine throne.

WHO ARE THE ANGELS WHO PRESIDE OVER THE VARIOUS LEVELS OF HEAVEN?

First Heaven: Gabriel
Second Heaven: Zachariel and Raphael
Third Heaven: Anahel
Fourth Heaven: Michael
Fifth Heaven: Sandalphon
Sixth Heaven: Zachiel
Seventh Heaven: Cassiel[22]

As you can see, some of these angels and archangels certainly cannot "rest in their watches," for their tasks are many!

DO ANGELS LIVE IN HUMAN FORM?

Angels do not live in human form, although they have been known to take on human appearance when dealing with us. Their natural state is one of pure light and energy.

DO ANGELS LIVE IN THE SKY?

Ancient cultures used to associate the sky with the domain of the gods or of God. Today, we are taught that angels live on another plane of existence. Most of the time, we are unable to see or hear them. At special times, however, they are able to reach across from their dimension to ours and comfort us or guide us as needed.

DO ANGELS LIVE IN HOUSES?

Angels do not require shelter from the elements, nor protection from each other the way human beings do. Nor do angels have a sense of possession or "owning stuff," the way that we consider owning numerous possessions an achievement.

The only home angels need is heaven, near the throne of God.

WHERE DO ANGELS SLEEP?

Modern literature and art have shown angels cuddled up on a soft cloud, catching up on their beauty rest. But angels actually have no need to sleep. As angels are beings of pure energy, their "bodies" do not need replenishing. According to the Bible, they "never rest in their watches."

DO ANGELS EAT?

Angels do not need to eat as we do for bodily sustenance, but they have been known to do so with their human friends when the occasion calls for it.

According to Gen. 18:1-16, three men came to visit Abraham at his tent by the oaks of Mamre, an ancient sacred place south of Jerusalem. Abraham greeted them royally, washing their feet and preparing a feast of fresh bread and cakes, a roast calf and cheese and milk. After they had eaten, the angels announced to Sarah, Abraham's wife, that she would have a son. Now Sarah thought this was highly unlikely, as she was past childbearing age. In fact, she could hardly keep from laughing out loud. But the angels' words were realized and the son she bore was known as Isaac, meaning "he laughs."

After their feast, the angels presumably were refortified for their next adventure. They left Abraham and his wife Sarah and went off to destroy the cities of Sodom and Gomorrah.

WHAT IS "ANGEL FOOD"?

We've all heard of angel food cake, angel hair pasta, or perhaps angels-on-horseback (savory of oysters wrapped in pieces of bacon), but there is one food actually associated with angels. During the years of wandering in the desert after fleeing from their captivity in Egypt, the Israelites were fed "manna" from heaven. "Manna" actually means "What is it?" which is what the Hebrews asked when they saw the food lying on the ground in the morning. It was thin and flaky and tasted like honey cakes.

Researchers now believe that manna is a nourishing substance excreted by plant lice that hardens in the dry air. But in ancient Jewish folklore, manna is the food of angels.

CAN ANGELS HAVE SPECIAL ANGEL FRIENDS?

Angels Gabriel and Michael are often reported to appear together. When people do see several angels together, the beings are sharing a joyous experience. One scholar was delighted to see several angels hovering over a group of trees, appearing to enjoy themselves immensely, and changing hues as they communicated.

DO ANGELS GO TO SCHOOL?

Angels do go to school in the sense that they are always evolving, always learning. In many ways, Earth is their schoolground, as they are made aware of the many nuances of human living. As human beings have evolved in knowledge, different problems arise. We have pollution of the waters, air and land, nuclear disasters, endangered species and high crime statistics.

We can only hope that our angels learn well and quickly. For sometimes it seems that only divine intervention will enable us to get out of the difficulties we have gotten ourselves into!

DO ANGELS EVER TAKE A HOLIDAY?

Some people believe that angels do take "holidays," which may explain why they aren't around when we need them the most. I am of the opposite opinion; I believe that our angels never leave us. I am reminded of the poem which asked of the Lord:

Lord, you said that once
I decided to follow you, you'd walk with me all the way.
Why at the troublesome times of my life,
the times I needed you most, would you leave me?

The Lord replied, "My precious child,
I love you and I would never, never leave you.
During your times of trial and suffering when you
saw only one set of footprints. . . .
That was when I carried you."

Author unknown, *Footprints*

In honor of our faithful angels, we have holidays just for them. October 2 is the day for guardian angels in the Roman Catholic Church, and September 29 is the feast day for Michael, Gabriel and Raphael. In England, there is a church holiday for Michael called Michaelmas, and in the Ethiopian and Egyptian Orthodox Churches, July 28 is the feast day for Uriel.

HAVE ANGELS EVER MARRIED?

In all the writings about angels, no one has ever come across a married angel. And a story in the Gospel of Saint Matthew implies that angels do not marry.

According to Matt. 22:23-30, the Sadducees (a group of priests) came to Jesus one day asking about the Resurrection, which they did not believe in. "Teacher," they said, "Moses told us that if a man dies and has no children, his brother must marry his widow. Now if this happens to seven brothers, whose wife will the woman be in heaven?" The Sadducees were pretty satisfied with themselves, thinking that they had silenced the Teacher.

But Jesus answered them by saying, "You are wrong, because you know neither the scriptures nor the power of God. For in the Resurrection they neither marry nor are given in marriage, but are like angels in heaven."

The sacrament of marriage was primarily given for the procreation of children, in order to continue the species. If human beings did not die, there would be no need to have children. In fact, it would get awfully crowded down here!

DO ANGELS HAVE SEX?

Certainly we are told that demons can and do have sex with each other and with mortal beings. Lilith, the Queen of Devils in Jewish lore, had sexual relations with the fallen angel Lucifer and the demon Asmodeus and attempted to seduce mortal men (often succeeding!). But do "good" angels have sex?

In John Milton's *Paradise Lost*, angels make love joyously:

Easier than Air with Air, if Spirits embrace,
Total they mix, Union of Pure with Pure
Desiring: nor restrain'd conveyance need
As Flesh to mix with Flesh, or Soul with Soul.

(8.626–629)

In Christian tradition, angels are sexless, taking on whatever human form they need to perform the duty at hand. If angels do make love, it is certainly not as physically experienced here on earth. Their own rapture exceeds earthly bounds and their ecstasy is beyond our understanding.

WHAT MUSICAL INSTRUMENTS ARE LINKED WITH ANGELS?

When you think about heaven, what do your senses tell you? Do you see radiant white light? Do you smell the wonderful aroma of flowers? Do you hear music?

A few instruments in particular have become associated with the angelic realm, depending on the occasion. We expect an angel with a trumpet to herald news of great import from God, and we find the music of the flute hauntingly exquisite. But the instrument most often connected with angels is the celestial harp, as many great artists have portrayed. In art, harps and other musical instruments represent the ethereal, beautiful music that many mystics and saints have reported hearing during angel visitations.

DO ANGELS SING?

It is impossible to think of angels and not think of singing. The Bible says that there is a troop of angels whose sole purpose is to gather around the throne of God in constant adoration, singing praises of great joy.

Heaven is a place dominated by great joy. In fact, Handel reported hearing heavenly voices singing while he was writing the Hallelujah chorus for the *Messiah*. And King George II was so powerfully affected when he heard the *Messiah* sung for the first time that he immediately sprang to his feet, standing throughout the chorus and starting a tradition that lasts today.

People who have experienced near-death trauma often report hearing heavenly music. And others have heard beautiful music from no apparent source while attending a funeral.

CHAPTER FOUR

WHAT IS THE HIERARCHY OF ANGELS?

WE TRUST, IN PLUMED PROCESSION,
FOR SUCH THE ANGELS GO,
RANK AFTER RANK, WITH EVEN FEET
AND UNIFORMS OF SNOW.

—EMILY DICKINSON

WHY IS THERE A HIERARCHY OF ANGELS?

Biblical accounts tell of various orders of angels, and medieval man believed that there were innumerable angels in the heavens. How could one possibly keep track of all the divine beings?

Long ago, it was decided that angels must be divided into a strict hierarchy, into which each angel would be assigned. This hierarchy was modeled after the existing feudal system, where feudal lords ruled large tracts of land.

Many different people came up with ideas of how heaven might be ordered, but the dispute ended with two publications: Saint Thomas Aquinas' proposed discourses, and the immortal work by the Italian poet Dante Alighieri, *The Divine Comedy*. Both men based their hierarchies of heaven on the work of Pseudo-Dionysius, a 6th century Greek writer. His writings on angels—including *The Celestial Hierarchy* and *The Ecclesiastical Hierarchy*—were originally thought to have been written by Dionysius the Areopagite, a 1st century Greek who converted to Christianity.

HOW ARE ANGELS RANKED?

The angels are ranked into three groupings:

1. Seraphim, cherubim and thrones
2. Dominions, virtues and powers
3. Principalities, archangels and angels

Listed below is a ranking of the angels. (The rulership of each category is debatable, due to differences of opinion among religious authorities.)

SERAPHIM

The seraphim are the highest order of angelic beings. They surround the throne of God and unceasingly sing, "Holy, holy, holy." They are the angels of love, of light and of fire and are depicted as having four faces and six wings. There are various angels who are said to rule the seraphim, possibly Seraphiel, Jehoel, Metatron, Michael or Satan, before his fall. Supposedly some of the order of the seraphim fell with Satan during the great rebellion.

CHERUBIM

Cherubim, the first angels to be mentioned in the Bible, were the angels who guarded the Garden of Eden from Adam and Eve. Cherubim of gold were also placed on the ark of the covenant, one on either side. In early Muslim lore, it was claimed that the cherubim were formed from the tears Michael shed over the sins of the faithful. The name and concept of the cherubim comes from Assyria, where they were pictured as huge, winged creatures, half man, half beast. In Rev. 4:8, John refers to the cherubim as six-winged and "full of eyes around and within." As you can see, these have little in common with our later concept of cherub! The chief ruler is said to be either Ophaniel, Rikbiel, Cherubiel, Raphael, Gabriel, Zophiel or Satan before his fall.

THRONES

The predominant characteristics of the thrones are virtue and steadfastness. According to Dionysius, it is through the thrones that "God brings his justice to bear upon us." The ruling prince of this order is said to be Oriphiel, Zadkiel or Zaphkiel.

DOMINIONS

Dionysius says of this group, "They regulate angels' duties and are perpetually aspiring to true lordship; through them the majesty of God is manifested." Dominions have been given scepters and orbs as symbols of their authority. The chief ruler is said to be Hashmal or Zadkiel.

VIRTUES

The virtues' principal duty is to work miracles on earth. They are known as bestowers of grace and valor. The two angels who accompanied Jesus during his ascension are believed to belong to the order of virtues. Their ruler is said to be either Michael, Raphael, Barbiel, Uzziel, Peliel or Satan before his fall.

POWERS

The powers' chief task is to ensure that heaven is orderly. Dionysius tells us that they prevent the overthrow of the world by demons. And some believe that these were the first angels to be created. Either Samael or Camael is considered the ruling prince.

PRINCIPALITIES

The principalities not only protect religion, but also watch over the rulers of the world, hopefully to help them rule wisely and well. The angel who rules this order is Requel, Anael, Haniel, Cerviel or Nisroc.

ARCHANGELS

Archangels are special messengers of God who appear at significant times, bearing the word of God to humankind. They also, according to the Testament of Levi, "minister and make propitiation to the Lord for the sins of ignorance and of the righteous." The ruling prince of the archangels is said to be either Michael or Raphael.

ANGELS

Angels are the lowest in this hierarchy. Their task is to watch over humankind and take care of animals, plants and other living things. Some of the angels reputed to have the top spot on the angelic order are Phaleg, Adnachiel, Gabriel and Chayyliel.

WHAT ARE WATCHERS AND HOLY ONES?

Perhaps you remember singing the hymn at church "Ye Watchers and Ye Holy Ones" and have wondered what exactly these are? The Watchers, or "grigori," are not mentioned in the hierarchy of angels, yet they are a high order of angels. They dwell in the fifth heaven.

Apparently, these angels were sent by God to instruct the children of men, but some were tempted by mortal women and began living with them. Those who did so became part of the fallen angels. Among the ranks of the "good" watchers (those who did not lust after earthy women) are Uriel, Raphael, Raguel, Michael, Zerachiel, Gabriel and Remiel. "Holy Ones" are simply angels.

WHO ARE THE SEVEN ARCHANGELS WHO STAND BEFORE GOD?

This has been a matter of great debate through the ages. Most church authorities agree on four of the great archangels: Michael, Gabriel, Raphael and Uriel. Chamuel, Jophiel and Zadkiel are also commonly included among the Seven Archangels who stand before God.

CHAPTER FIVE

WHERE DO ANGELS COME FROM?

IT IS SAID, AND IT IS TRUE, THAT JUST BEFORE WE ARE BORN A CAVERN ANGEL PUTS HIS FINGER TO OUR LIPS AND SAYS, "HUSH, DON'T TELL WHAT YOU KNOW." THIS IS WHY WE ARE BORN WITH A CLEFT ON OUR UPPER LIPS AND REMEMBERING NOTHING OF WHERE WE CAME.

—RODERICK MACLEISH, *PRINCE OMBRA*

WHEN AND WHERE IS THE FIRST MENTION OF AN ANGEL RECORDED?

The first mention of angels in the Bible is in Gen. 3:22-24.

Once Adam and Eve had succumbed to temptation and eaten of the fruit of the tree of life, God drove them out of the Garden of Eden. God said, "Behold, the man has become like 'one of us', knowing good and evil; and now, lest he put forth his hand and take also of the tree of life, and eat, and live for ever." God sent them from the garden. Some scholars believe that the phrase 'one of us' refers to all the divine beings in the heavens.

But, more important, it is reported in the Bible that God stationed cherubim at the entrance to the gates, thereby ensuring that humans would never again enter the garden. Thus, the cherubim are the first of the heavenly hierarchy to be named.

ARE THERE MANY ANGELS MENTIONED IN THE BIBLE?

Despite over 375 references to angels in the Bible, specific names of angels are rarely mentioned. Most of our knowledge of angels comes from two collections of works, the Apocrypha and the Pseudepigrapha. The books in these collections were written primarily between the time of the last book of the Old Testament and the books of the New Testament (approximately 200 B.C. to A.D. 100). The Book of Jubilees, in the Apocrypha, was said to have been dictated to Moses by an angel, and describes the history of the world from its creation.

During the Reformation, the Church Fathers set about the task of creating a book for their followers. The books of the Apocrypha and the Pseudepigrapha were pronounced to be less divinely inspired than other books and were omitted from the Bible as we know it today. Many books written shortly after the time of Christ were also declined entrance. Some of these are known as the Gnostic Gospels. There are also many more works that have been revealed in the Dead Sea Scrolls, which were found in caves by the Dead Sea in 1947.

Our knowledge of angels comes from many sources besides the Bible. These include mystical books, which have been considered too complex for most people to understand, and works of poetry and literature.

WERE ANY RELIGIONS "STARTED" BY ANGELS?

There are two famous cases of angels changing the course of history and causing men to turn to a new way of worshipping their Lord.

The most renowned is, of course, the revelation that the archangel Gabriel gave to the Prophet Mohammed, on a night that has come to be known as the Night of Power and Glory. Gabriel (or Jibril, as he is known in Islam) revealed the Koran to the mighty Prophet, and between Gabriel's eyes were written the words that are the foundation of Islam: "There is No God but Allah, and Mohammed is His Prophet." This vision was the beginning of the great religion of Islam, which today has spread around the world. In the Koran, Jesus himself (or Isa) is included in the company of angels.

In 1827, at Hill Cumorah, New York, Joseph Smith claimed that the angel Moroni led him to the gold plates that contained "the gospel of the new revelation," the Book of Mormon. Later, followers of this new religion would build a great Tabernacle in Salt Lake City, Utah, and become known as the Church of Latter Day Saints.

DO BOOKS OTHER THAN THE BIBLE TALK ABOUT ANGELS?

There are many books that describe angels and their everyday tasks. When Gustav Davidson wrote *A Dictionary of Angels,* he examined numerous other writings, some ancient and others modern, to compile his exhaustive list of angelic names. Among some of his sources are:

The Apocryphal New Testament
The Book of Mormon
The Kabbalah
The Apocrypha and Pseudepigrapha of the Old Testament
The Koran
The Dead Sea Scrolls

DO PEOPLE OTHER THAN CHRISTIANS BELIEVE IN ANGELS?

Yes, angels appear prominently in Jewish and Islamic belief systems. In fact, some angels even have the same names. Gabriel is a beloved archangel for the Christian, Jew and Muslim, as is Michael. Islamic mystics, known as Sufis, claim that angels are the companions of our hearts and reflect the love of God.

Many ancient religions believed in great winged beings; the Romans and Greeks depicted some of their gods with wings. Other modern-day religions also have supernatural beings who intercede for humankind and bring messages from the divine.

The following is a listing of various groups and their belief in supernatural beings.

NATIVE AMERICANS

The Native Americans had contact with white Europeans centuries ago. Many of the early Europeans who came to the New World wanted to convert the "heathen" to the ways of the Church. In the 1640s, Saint Jean de Brébeuf wrote the *Huron Carol*, a haunting Christmas carol for his early converts. A 20th century Native American painting shows two winged Indian spirits coming for the Indian Chief Black Elk at his death.

But before the coming of the white man, and in the native traditions handed down today, Raven and Eagle are the winged messengers from God. These "spirit animals" can see very far and fly very high—very close to God Himself. Both these winged messengers bring knowledge, protection and warnings to their people.

PUEBLO INDIANS

Traditionally, the Indians of the American southwest believe in life spirits called Kachina, which gently, lovingly guide them. These spirits are sometimes depicted in Pueblo art as having bird-like qualities. Dolls representing the Kachina spirits are used to bring good luck and healing to the needy.

ZOROASTRIANS

The prophet Zoroaster lived between 1000 and 600 B.C. He introduced the concept of one God, Ahura Mazda, to the Babylonians. Ahura Mazda was in constant conflict with the evil spirit, Angra Mainyu, and was helped in his struggle by seven archangels.

Zoroastrianism was the religion of the Babylonians during the captivity of the Israelites. It was the source of the concepts of good and evil, and of angels and archangels for the Jewish people, then in captivity.

At this time, the story of Shadrach, Meshach and Abednego originated. These men were holy men who obeyed God's will. Nebuchadnezzar grew angry with their faith and devotion to their Lord, and decided to rid his kingdom of them. He had them bound and thrown into a very hot fiery furnace. But, ac-

73

cording to Dan. 3:25, what the king saw astonished him: "I see four men loose, walking in the midst of the fire, and they are not hurt; and the appearance of the fourth is like a son of the gods." The fourth was an angel. Nebuchadnezzar was so impressed with what he saw, that he proclaimed their God should be spoken of with respect.

Today Zoroastrians mainly live in India, where they are called Parsees. Due to strict rules forbidding intermarriage, the sect is getting smaller and smaller.

HINDUS

In ancient Hinduism, there seems to be little concept of what we think of as angels. Perhaps the closest we can get are the "kinpuru'sh," winged beings who worship the gods. In modern Hindu practice, however, there are many angels. It is possible that the people of India were influenced by the early Western conquerors and settlers, who brought with them the concept of angels. The "pitarah," for example, are household spirits who guard the occupants from illness, famine and drought.

TAOISTS

There is no word for angel in Taoism, but Chinese and Japanese religions have beings who minister to the sick and infirm and worship the divine. They are known as "immortals," human beings who have reached such spiritual enlightenment that they never die. They perform angel-like duties such as miracles and healing and teaching of humankind. At times, immortals take on human or animal guise, traveling between worlds to give messages and advice to humans.

BUDDHISTS

Angelic beings are frequently shown surrounding Buddha or Bodhisattvas in Buddhist art. They are usually called "tennin" and are painted without wings, but with flowing garments representing flight. They are always depicted as feminine, with their hair arranged beautifully and set off with a small crown or ornamental wreath.

Temple paintings of these radiant beings can be found in Japan, Korea, India and Thailand. As in the Western tradition, they can often be seen singing songs of praise, playing musical instruments or carrying sacred banners.

CANADIAN INUIT

The Inuit of the central Arctic believe that every child has a guardian spirit who is the soul of one who has recently died. The child is addressed by that "Old One's" name until the child reaches an age when he or she begins to assume an individual personality.

Like the Native Americans, the Inuit worship Raven and Crow, as well as other animal spirits. Raven and Crow are the messengers between the Great Spirit and humankind.

CHAPTER SIX

WHAT DO THE ANGELS' NAMES MEAN?

MAKE YOURSELF FAMILIAR WITH THE ANGELS,
AND BEHOLD THEM FREQUENTLY IN SPIRIT;
FOR WITHOUT BEING SEEN,
THEY ARE PRESENT WITH YOU.

—SAINT FRANCES DE SALES

DO ALL ANGELS HAVE NAMES?

It is believed that all angels have names, for angels are individuals, just as we are. In many cases, however, we know angels by what they do, as the "Angel of Air" or the "Angel of Sun," rather than their proper name.

The names of angels first appeared in the book of Daniel, where Gabriel and Michael were mentioned. The Greeks later described groups of angels particularly close to God. These included Gabriel, Michael, Uriel and Raphael as the archangels.

HOW DO THEY GET THEIR NAMES?

The ancient Jews borrowed the names from the Persians and from the Babylonians during the period of their captivity. In fact, both Michael and Gabriel owe their names to Babylonian mythology. A number of angels, but certainly not all, have names ending in "el" or "irion," which means "of God." It is easy, then, to take a common word and make it angelic. Hod (or splendor) was the base word for the angel Hodiel, whose name can be translated as the "splendor of God."

I have concluded that angelic names still remain as much a mystery as does the name of the Lord. We have simply given them names in order to suitably identify them for our purposes. I suspect that the names of angels, when "spoken" by other celestial beings, are beautiful beyond our understanding.

DO THEIR NAMES HAVE ANY MEANING?

As we have seen above, most of the angelic names have a meaning somewhat similar to our own names. Here are a few angels' names with their meanings:

Araphie: neck of God
Boel: God is in him
Emmanuel: God with us
Iofiel: beauty of God
Hutriel: rod of God
Suriel: God's command
Za'afiel: wrath of God

DO ANGELS HAVE MORE THAN ONE NAME?

Some angels are known by different names by different groups of worship. For instance, the "Gabriel" of the Jews and Christians is called "Jibriel" by Muslims. But the angel with the most names is "Metatron," whom we met earlier as "Enoch." Metatron is actually known among numerous religious groups by over 100 names!

IS THERE A LISTING OF ANGEL NAMES?

The best source of angel names is Gustav Davidson's *A Dictionary of Angels*, published in 1967 after 15 years of exhaustive research. The explanation of each angelic name includes its meaning, where the angel is located, what tasks it may perform and other information. There is detailed information about the archangels, including short stories of their feats, plus the names of fallen angels.

CHAPTER SEVEN

WHO ARE THE MOST FAMOUS ANGELS?

HOW MANY ANGELS CAN DANCE ON THE POINT OF A
VERY FINE NEEDLE WITHOUT JOSTLING EACH OTHER?

—ISAAC D'ISRAELI, *CURIOSITIES OF LITERATURE*

WHO IS THE MOST FAMOUS ANGEL IN THE NEW TESTAMENT?

Certainly for most Christians, the most famous angel in the New Testament is Gabriel ("God is my strength"), who announced to Mary that she would bear a child called Jesus. It was after hearing this wonderful news that Mary rejoiced with the beautiful words known to us today as the "Magnificat."

Gabriel is not only a star of the New Testament, but he and Michael are the only two angels mentioned in the Old Testament. And, of course, Gabriel played a central role in the establishment of Islam.

Gabriel is the Angel of Annunciation, Resurrection, Mercy, Vengeance, Death and Revelation, and figures prominently in Jewish lore. He is the angel who destroyed the cities of Sodom and Gommorah and who wrestled with Jacob. He is a favorite subject for religious artists and poets as well as being one of the two highest-ranking angels in Judeo-Christian and Islamic traditions.

WHO IS THE MOST FAMOUS ANGEL IN THE MODERN MEDIA?

Clarence Oddbody from the movie *It's a Wonderful Life* appears to be the most famous angel, although some argue that Jonathan Smith (played by the late Michael Landon) of the TV series *Highway to Heaven* is better known. But for me, Christmas just hasn't happened until I've cried over *It's a Wonderful Life*. Clarence (played by Henry Travers) is a wonderful, bumbling angel trying to "earn his wings" by showing the desperate, suicidal George Bailey (James Stewart) how important his life has been to those around him.

Happily, George is convinced of the worthiness of his life and returns to his family to "face the music." But the spirit of Christmas reigns supreme, good overcomes evil and Clarence gets his wings!

ARE THERE MANY FILMS FEATURING ANGELS?

Actually, there are more films featuring angels than you might suppose. Here's a list should you wish to rent some videos one weekend:

Angel on My Shoulder
The Bishop's Wife
Forever Darling
Heaven Can Wait
The Horn Blows at Midnight
It's a Wonderful Life
The Milagro Beanfield War
One Magic Christmas
Wings of Desire

Some people include *Ghost* and *Field of Dreams* in the angel category, although they are not strictly about angels. Another delight is the British TV series *Mr. Pye*.

WHICH ANGELS ARE THE BEST KNOWN TO HUMANKIND?

Without a doubt, the angels best known to us are our guardian angels. We deal with them on a daily basis, sometimes consciously, sometimes not. Sometimes they become visible to us at times of need or trouble. Throughout the ages, men and women have walked with their guardians, and there can be little doubt that these angels are the closest to us and we to them.

WHO ARE THE 10 BEST-KNOWN ANGELS OR ARCHANGELS?

The 10 best-known angels are:

Michael
Gabriel
Raphael
Uriel
Lucifer
Metatron
Ariel
Victor or Victorious
Logos
Moroni

MICHAEL ("WHO IS AS GOD")

Michael is surely the greatest of all angels, achieving this standing in Jewish, Christian and Islamic writings. He was the first angel to have a following when Constantine the Great (A.D. 280-337) erected a magnificent church to him

85

in his honor. Michael is master of the order of virtues, head of archangels, Prince of the Presence, Angel of Repentance, Righteousness, Mercy and Sanctification, ruler of the Fourth Heaven and guardian of Israel. But perhaps his best known deed is that of the dragon-slayer, now often associated with Saint George. In fact, an Old English gold coin bearing the figure of Michael piercing a dragon is called an "angel."

Legends have it that Michael was one of the angels who assisted at the burial of Moses, that as Saint Michael he led the souls of those who have died into eternal bliss, and that he was the angel who told Mary of her approaching death. He is one of the most frequently painted of all the angels, usually shown with wings and an unsheathed sword. One of the latest developments is that Pope Pius XII declared him to be the patron of police officers in 1950.

GABRIEL
("GOD IS MY STRENGTH")

After Michael, Gabriel is the highest-ranking angel in Jewish, Christian and Islamic tradition. Gabriel presides over heaven, is the Prince of Justice and the chief of the angelic guards. His name is Chaldean in origin, and the Israelites do not seem to have been acquainted with him before their captivity in Babylon. According to one legend, Gabriel once did not strictly obey a command from God and for this remained for awhile outside heaven. It was during this period that the angel Dobiel (guardian angel of Persia) stood in his place.

Gabriel is the bearer of great news and the most loved of messengers. He brought the news to Mary and to her cousin, Elizabeth, that they would both bear sons—Jesus and John the Baptist—who would change the course of history. And it was Gabriel who dictated the Koran to the Prophet Mohammed.

One can even get a glimpse of his footprint—Gabriel is the angel who is said to have visited Father George Rapp, the leader of the Second Advent community in New Harmony, Indiana. His footprint can be seen on a limestone slab in the garden of the Maclure-Owen home.

RAPHAEL
("GOD HAS HEALED")

Raphael is one of the most beloved, written about and painted angels. He is the Angel of the Sun, the guardian of the tree of life, an Angel of Prayer, Love, Joy and Light. Not only is he the Angel of Healing, he is also the Angel of Science and Knowledge. Rabbi Abba in the Zohar says, "Raphael is charged to heal the earth, and through him . . . the Earth furnishes an abode for man, whom also he heals of his maladies."[23] The Zohar is a 13th century work that describes Jewish mysticism, as does the Kabbalah, published in

1611. (The Hebrew word *cabala* means "received tradition.")

Legends about Raphael are numerous. According to lore, he was one of the three angels who visited Abraham (the others were Michael and Gabriel). He helped heal Jacob's leg after he injured it wrestling with a heavenly adversary, and gave Noah a medical book after the flood. Perhaps one of the most endearing images we have of Raphael from the works of the great masters is that of Raphael holding a pilgrim's staff.

URIEL
("FIRE OF GOD")

Uriel is one of the leading angels of God, highly esteemed in times past. He is said to be an Angel of the Presence (which ranks him among the highest of angels, being so close to God), watcher over Tartarus (or Hades), presider over thunder and terror, and, most importantly, the Archangel of Salvation.

Some have claimed that Uriel was one of the cherubim who stood guard at the gates of Eden after Adam and Eve had been driven out. He also is supposed to have been the messenger who was sent to warn Noah of the impending flood. Uriel is the Angel of September and thus may be called upon by those who are born in this month.

Like Michael, Uriel has been canonized by the Catholic Church. His symbol is an open hand holding a flame.

LUCIFER
("LIGHT GIVER")

The name Lucifer means "star" or "light giver" and originally applied to the morning or evening star, which is Venus. To early Church fathers, Lucifer was equated with Satan, and thus was given the role as the arch-enemy of humankind, the Prince of Hell. Before his fall, however, Lucifer was thought to be one of the most beloved angels of the Lord, seated beside Him, an Angel of Magnificence and Glory.

METATRON
("CLOSEST TO THE THRONE")

As mentioned previously, Metatron is one of the most mysterious of all the angels, and in noncanonical works is considered the greatest of all the angels. His presence is overwhelming. When invoked, he can appear as a pillar of fire, his face more dazzling than the sun. Perhaps one of his more touching roles, according to the Talmud, is that of teacher to the children who are in heaven.

An interesting explanation for the transformation of Enoch into Metatron exists in the Zohar. When God created Adam, He put into his body a divine spark. But once Adam sinned, he lost that gift, which then entered Enoch. Enoch was thus able to attain spiritual perfection. As that is deemed impossible for mere mortals, he was lifted up to heaven, becoming the angel Metatron.

Outside Biblical tradition, Metatron is perhaps the greatest of all the heavenly beings. He is known as the king of angels, Prince of the Divine Face or Presence, chancellor of heaven, Angel of the Covenant, chief of the ministering angels, and the lesser YHWH. Metatron was the patriarch Enoch who was taken into heaven, and for students of the Talmud, he represents a link between God and man. (The Talmud is a collection of writings by great rabbis penned between the years A.D. 200 and 500.)

The name Metatron has never been explained to the satisfaction of Biblical scholars. The most plausible meaning suggested would be "one who occupies the throne next to the divine throne." And, according to the Kabbalah (a history of Jewish mysticism), Metatron is the angel who led the children of Israel through the wilderness. He is the tallest of the angels, with multiple tasks and duties. Among other tasks, he is the angel to whom God gives daily orders as to which souls will be taken up into heaven that day. He then delegates this to his subordinates. Or perhaps he uses one of his 100 aliases to accomplish the job!

ARIEL
("LION OF GOD")

Perhaps Ariel is now most famous for his role in Shakespeare's *The Tempest,* an airy sprite who does the bidding of Prospero, the Duke of Milan. Ariel's most memorable lines are:

Where the bee sucks, there suck I
In a cowslip's bell I lie;
There I couch when owls do cry,
On the bat's back I do fly
After the summer merrily:
Merrily, merrily shall I live now
Under the blossom that hangs on the bough.

(5.1.88–94)

Jewish mystics have used Ariel in poetry as a name for Jerusalem. And Thomas Heywood in his *The Hierarchy of the Blessèd Angels,* published in 1635, says that Ariel is the "Earth's great Lord." Some of Ariel's greater works are performed when he is assisting the angel Raphael on missions of healing.

VICTOR OR VICTORIOUS

The angel Victorious is most likely the best known angel in Ireland. Legend has it that this angel appeared to Saint Patrick and requested that he return to Ireland to convert the pagans to Christianity. Saint Patrick reported daily conversations with this angel, who could also be described as Saint Patrick's own guardian angel.

LOGOS
("WORD")

Some consider the Logos (or the "word") to be the oldest angel, the angel made in the image of God. We might also think of the Logos as being the personal guardian angel of God.

Most Christians are familiar with John 1:1–5: "In the beginning was the Word, and the Word was with God, and the Word was God. He was in the beginning with God; all things were made through him, and without him was not anything made that was made. In him was life, and the life was the light of men. The light shines in the darkness, and the darkness has not overcome it."

MORONI

The angel Moroni visited Joseph Smith, the founder of the Church of Latter Day Saints, and led Smith to discover the buried golden plates that contained a detailed account of a forgotten history of North America.

According to this history, a Jewish family fled Jerusalem before its destruction, making its way to the new continent. One line of the descendants of these people became the native peoples of North America. Another line was lost and vanished from history. An elder of these lost people, named Mormon, recorded that Jesus appeared to them after the Resurrection, and his son, Moroni, buried the golden plates that were later revealed to Joseph Smith, founder of the Church of the Latter Day Saints.

The story goes on to say that Moroni was transformed into an angel and later helped Smith translate these records, which became the Book of Mormon.

WHO IS THE ANGEL OF THE LORD?

Sometimes the Angel of the Lord is God Himself, especially in earlier books of the Old Testament, but other times it appears that He sends various angels to do His bidding. Michael, Metatron and Gabriel, among others, have been referred to as the "Angel of the Lord."

In the New Testament, in Acts 12:1-7, Saint Peter is released from prison by an angel of the Lord. King Herod (the grandson of Herod the Great) had killed James, the brother of John, and had his soldiers arrest and imprison Peter during the celebration of the Passover. But the night that Herod was going to bring Peter out to his death, the angel of the Lord appeared to Peter, opening the gates and causing the guards to be paralyzed. Peter fled to the house of friends who initially refused to let him in, believing that it was his angel knocking at the door. In those times, people believed that a person's guardian angel represented him in heaven.

The Angel of the Lord saved Isaac from sacrifice, appeared to Moses in the burning bush and was seen by Balsam's donkey to warn of impending danger. The angel has also appeared as an adversary acting for the Lord.

WHO IS THE ANGEL OF DEATH?

The Angel of Death does God's bidding, and usually is not considered to be a fallen or evil angel. In fact, he actually may be several angels to whom Metatron delegates! For Christians, the Angel of Death is Michael, who helps to guide them into the light of eternal life. For Arabs, he is Azrael, and for Jews he is any one of a dozen or more, including Adriel, Gabriel and Metatron.

Some people believe that it was the Angel of Death who killed all the first-born male children of the Egyptians, the last of the plagues leading to the Exodus. But the Biblical reading states that it was the Lord who carried out this work on His own. Apocryphal writings are the best source of information on this angel, who was often considered to be kindly and benevolent, helpful and caring to the human souls he guided.

WHO IS THE ANGEL OF MERCY?

The two angels that have been mentioned for this honor are Gabriel and Michael. But by far the most interesting angel is Rhamiel. Rhamiel was Saint Francis of Assisi, lover of all animals and a healer before his transformation to the angelic realm!

WHO IS REFERRED TO AS THE ANGEL OF THE MORNING?

Numerous angels are assigned the task of keeping watch over the hours of each day. On Sundays, for instance, Michael can be found taking the eight o'clock watch. But somehow I think that the "angels" referred to in this popular song, written by C. Taylor, are the wives and mothers who are up early preparing breakfast and lunches for their loved ones. This is truly an angelic endeavor!

CHAPTER EIGHT

WHAT ARE GUARDIAN ANGELS?

Sweet souls around us watch us still
Press nearer to our side;
Into our thoughts, into our prayers,
With gentle helpings glide.

—Harriet Beecher Stowe, *In the Other World*

WHAT ARE GUARDIAN ANGELS?

Guardian angels are a group of angels who have dedicated themselves to the task of helping humankind directly, by guiding the life of one person. There are those who claim to have met their angel, know his name and converse with him regularly about their everyday needs and desires. Guardian angels are like our best friends. They are always there in time of need, to laugh with you in playful times, hold your hand when you think you can't take another step, celebrate your victories and wipe away your tears. And, no matter what you may do or say, their love for you is unconditional.

Because the word "guardian" makes one think of danger, some have chosen to call the guardian angel a "companion angel." It doesn't really matter. Whatever you choose to call your angel, you know that he is with you, hovering just over your shoulder, whispering in your ear. Perhaps you feel an itch on your nose? It could just be your angel trying to get your attention!

DOES EVERYONE HAVE A GUARDIAN ANGEL?

Everyone has a guardian angel whether we believe in angels or not. They watch over us, protect us from harm, comfort us in times of sorrow.

Sophy Burnham's book, *Angel Letters*, is a collection of letters written by people who have experienced their guardian angels first hand. They tell of angels bringing peace to the dying, warning of accidents on the road ahead, replacing a flat tire, healing the sick. And, as these letters reveal, it doesn't matter what religion you follow: Guardian angels are known by Catholics, Jews, Muslims, Protestants, and Buddhists. Guardian angels have no prejudices or cultural sensitivities. To them, we are just human beings with the need to be loved.

WHEN DO WE GET OUR GUARDIAN ANGELS?

Guardian angels are with us from the time of our birth. What we don't know is if they are with us before that moment. Some people who believe in reincarnation think that angels guide our souls to choose the "right" parents and experiences in this lifetime. Others believe that our angels decide to be our guardians and help us get used to this new world at the instant we open our eyes.

IS IT POSSIBLE TO HAVE MORE THAN ONE GUARDIAN ANGEL?

It has never been reported that a person had more than one guardian angel. However, more than one angel may visit or help an individual. In special times, other angels may help the guardian angel.

DO OUR GUARDIAN ANGELS MEET US WHEN WE DIE?

Our guardian angels are with us always. They especially help us pass over the threshold of death, for they are acutely aware that many of us are afraid of dying. Often, they will reveal themselves before a person dies, to strengthen the person who is dying and comfort those who will be left behind.

Melissa Deal Forth of Atlanta, Georgia, told of her experience in Angel Letters. *Her husband, Chris, was in the hospital undergoing chemotherapy for acute lymphatic leukemia. He was a very sick man, with tubes running in and out of his body and little strength to move. One night, Chris woke up suddenly and felt compelled to leave his bed and go to the chapel. He somehow managed this without waking Melissa, who was in the same room sleeping on a cot, and walked by the nurses' station without being seen. In the chapel he met a man in a red-checked flannel shirt, blue jeans and brand new lace-up work boots. The two talked for some time, with the stranger comforting Chris, letting him know that all his prayers had been answered. Melissa found Chris in the chapel after a frantic search, and was amazed to see this stranger who had somehow gotten past security into the hospital. But, at Chris' request, she left them to continue their conversation alone. Afterwards, Chris was full of life and energy. "Melissa," he said, "he was an angel." Chris died a few days later.*[24]

People who have had near-death experiences have reported conversing with beautiful beings surrounded by white light and feeling absolute love and understanding. Many have said that their lives changed for the better afterwards, and the love and peace they felt stayed with them. Can there be any doubt that our angels who watch over us in life, comfort and protect us in death?

WHY DO "BAD" THINGS HAPPEN TO GOOD PEOPLE IF WE HAVE GUARDIAN ANGELS TO PROTECT US?

I remember asking my minister when I was a little girl why I had not received something I had prayed so very hard for. And his answer was that "God answers all prayers. But sometimes His answer is 'No.'"

It is also very upsetting for us to see someone we love suffer, especially when that person is loving and caring. But often we come to realize that the suffering itself serves to strengthen and uplift. The "bad" things give us the ability to reach down deep inside ourselves and become even better. Later, we are able to understand and help others even more.

Our guardian angels respect that humans have been given free will, just like themselves, and that tragedy in our lives gives us the opportunity to grow. But there can be no doubt that our angels surround us in times of need and feel our suffering.

The film, *Wings of Desire*, shows most poignantly how our angels long to protect us from harm, but always bow to human will. In this movie, the angel is unable to stop a man from committing suicide by jumping off a bridge and we, as the audience, feel his grief. Angels walk beside us in good times and bad, sharing both our joys and sorrows.

DO "BAD" PEOPLE HAVE GUARDIAN ANGELS?

All of us are under the protection of guardian angels. Even those people we consider "bad"—criminals, murderers, outcasts from society, anyone who intentionally hurts another person. But all angels respect our God-given right to free will. They wait in the hope that someday their charges will want to turn their lives around. When this happens, the angels will be there to help in full force. Jesus talked of this when he spoke of the parable of the wayward son.

Once, long ago, a man had two sons. The younger son squandered what his father had given him in loose living, wandering the countryside. When a great famine came over the land, and the son was hungry, he returned home to his father and begged his forgiveness, saying that he was not worthy to be called his son. The father rejoiced and had a great feast to celebrate the return of his lost son. The older son, however, was angry. He had spent his time serving his father and obeying his commands. But, according to Luke 15:31-32, his father told him, "Son, you are always with me, and all that is mine is yours. It was fitting to make merry and be glad, for your brother was lost and now he is found." And Jesus had started the story by saying, "Just so I tell you, there is joy before the angels of God over one sinner who repents."

Some believe that we have two angels, one good and one bad. Perhaps you recall cartoons with a little demon on one side of the cartoon character and a cute angel on the other? The "bad" angel whispers all those things we know we shouldn't do; the "good" angel gives us good advice. The more we listen to the "demon within," the more "wrong" things we do and it becomes harder and harder to do good. And, of course, the opposite happens if we listen to our good angel. Even though we may have all the help of our guardian angels at our beckoning, only we can choose the course of our lives.

WHAT DO OUR GUARDIAN ANGELS EXPECT IN RETURN?

Our guardian angels expect nothing in return from us. There is no bartering system, much as we may think. I wonder how many times we might have said, "If you do this for me, I promise I'll be good for the rest of my life."

We might ask of ourselves to be the best that we can, to live each moment to the fullest, to strive to be helpful, loving beings. But our angels don't ask that of us. They simply encourage.

ARE GUARDIAN ANGELS HEALERS?

Like all the other angels and archangels, guardian angels cannot heal. But they do bring healing messages from God. By using prayer and meditation, we facilitate the healing process within us.

CAN MY GUARDIAN ANGEL BE THE GUARDIAN ANGEL OF SOMEONE ELSE?

There are more angels in heaven than there are people on the face of this earth. Every one of us has a guardian angel, who arrives promptly around the time of our birth. But while each angel may be different, some angels may have the same names or the same attributes, and thus might be mistaken as the same angel.

We can rest assured that our angels are always with us. They don't have to leave when a call comes from another person. All the evidence suggests that our angels are always available, eager and willing to help.

CAN ARCHANGELS BE GUARDIAN ANGELS?

Certainly it is possible. We know that Michael, for example, was the guardian of Jacob. Archangels do seem to confine themselves to other tasks and act as guardians to persons of great import. But that doesn't mean that one couldn't be your guardian angel!

WILL MY GUARDIAN ANGEL HELP ME WIN THE LOTTERY?

Everything happens for a reason. And that reason may be to learn a lesson—or perhaps, to have all the money we need to realize our full potential in life! We could use a windfall to help others or establish a trust for the needy.

I don't believe that wishful entreaties to your guardian angel will result in a million-dollar winning ticket. But if winning the lottery is your destiny, then your angel will no doubt speed the process. For the rest of us, perhaps *not* winning the lottery is the lesson.

WHO BELIEVES IN GUARDIAN ANGELS?

We know that almost every religion on earth has a belief that there are spirits who protect them and their households. And the Judeo-Christian tradition maintains that guardian angels are a guiding influence on the lives of each one of us.

Little children seem to be especially connected to the angelic realm. You probably know little ones who play with "invisible friends" or tell of talking to people who visit them in the night. Adults often dismiss these as cute childhood fantasies. In time, children begin to doubt their experiences, and grow up forgetting their childhood friends and helpers. They start to wonder, "Are there really angels?"

We can now answer, "Yes. And we know that they are with us from the moment we take our first breath." I believe that our lives are made a little bit easier by the knowledge that we are constantly surrounded by love.

CHAPTER NINE

WHAT DO CHILDREN THINK OF ANGELS?

THE THIRD-GRADE ANGELS, TWO BY TWO
MARCH IN, THEIR CARDBOARD WINGS ASKEW.

—MARGARET FISHBACK ANTOLINI, *CHRISTMAS PAGEANT*

As Art Linkletter once remarked, children say the darnedest things. And too often the adults of this world simply dismiss their stories as mere fantasies. I decided to find out from children what they thought about angels and to see if they had any questions. But in fact, the children I encountered were so absorbed in telling me about angels that very few thought of any questions! I was intrigued that so many of the children had an invisible friend. Perhaps these were the children's guardian angels.

STEPHANIE
(AGE 8)

I had an invisible friend when I was seven. Her name was Kara. I really liked her a lot. She always wanted to race me to my bike when I played outside.

I have seen many, many angels, some were in the Bible and some were in stories and in movies.

I think an angel has a white dress, a golden halo in its hair. They have white slippers. I think angels watch over you and me. They take good care of you. A lot of people go to church. There are angels there who watch over you.

Stephanie also wrote a poem:

There are beautiful Angels up in the Heaven,
They watch over us morning, noon and at seven.

They are all dressed in white from their heads to their shoes,
And they are always ready to share the "Good News."
They look just like fairies with a golden halo in their hair,
And their hands are folded ready for prayer.

Her question is:

DO YOU THINK ANGELS WEAR CLOTHES?

Yes, Stephanie, I do think that angels wear clothes when they appear to us in human form. And very likely you would see an angel just as you described, in white flowing robes with matching slippers.

It is possible that some of your friends may see angels differently—perhaps in a flannel shirt and jeans or in a three-piece suit. No matter how it looks, I'm sure you'll know your angel!

JAMIE
(AGE 8)

I had an invisible friend when I was five. His name was Plucky.

I think an angel looks like this: It has a long dress, wings, a gold circle a little above their heads, and are skinny and fat.

CHERI
(AGE 7)

I think an angel has wings and wears a white robe, and on his head he wears a halo. Girl angels dress the same.

I think angels guard me and tell me to do the right things.

RYAN
(AGE 8)

I think an angel looks like a bird with white, big shoes and hands and wings. They wear a white suit. They can be boys or girls. They help people when they are in trouble.

SHAWN
(AGE 7)

Angels are invisible. They have two white wings, blue eyes and come in different sizes. Angels play games like Monopoly with other angels. Angels fly to God.

SHAYNE
(AGE 8)

I think an angel looks like this: He has a yellow ring around his head and a white body. Angels like to do things for people.

An angel has helped me by giving me help in church and giving me his blessing.

ANDREA
(AGE 8)

My invisible friend is a unicorn. Her name is Diamond. She is white with light pink wings.

I have seen an angel in my old house. She came every night through my window and we would talk. Angels are pretty nice, helpful and kind to people.

KIMBERLY
(AGE 7)

I think an angel looks like it has all white clothes, long or short hair, a gold ring around his head, shoes and red lips. Angels take care of us. When my auntie died it helped me not to cry very much.

KEITH
(AGE 7)

I have an invisible friend. He has a jean jacket and he has a pair of jeans on.

I have seen angels when I was decorating my Christmas tree. I looked out the window and saw it. It had two white wings, silver dress, and something gold around its head. It was slowly flying in front of my window. Maybe it was talking to Santa. I liked watching it but I couldn't tell if it was a boy or a girl. It made me feel good. Maybe their job is to visit people at Christmas.

I was climbing a tree and fell but an angel put me on a branch. I didn't fall all the way down. I didn't get hurt. I could feel the angel carrying me.

COLT
(AGE 7)

I have an invisible friend. His name is Guy. He is very tall, as tall as anybody can be. He is very old, about 50 years old. He plays games with me, like puzzles. He lives in an apartment in Toronto. He rides on his motor bike to come and see me.

I have seen angels in the Bible and in a movie called *Date With an Angel.*

An angel has a person's body and has two goldish wings. They can be a boy or a girl. If it's a girl they have blue eyes with goldish-brown hair. Some were bad and some were good. The bad angel has black wings and has a sword. Boy angels look like girl angels but they have shorter hair. They save peoples' lives.

Colt has two questions:

HOW FAR UP ARE THEY?

Angels live very far up, Colt, because they live in heaven. And we think of heaven as being very far away, because we can't see it. Imagine you are blindfolded and can't see what is all around you. You might think that the next room is very far away because you can't see it.

HOW DO ANGELS LIVE FOREVER?

Angels live forever because they do not have physical bodies like we do. They never die. But even though our body dies, our soul lives on forever. Angels are like our souls.

CHAPTER TEN

WHAT ARE FALLEN ANGELS?

AN ANGEL WAS TIRED OF HEAVEN, AS HE LOUNGED IN
THE GOLDEN STREET; HIS HALO WAS TILTED SIDEWAYS,
AND HIS HARP LAY MUTE AT HIS FEET; SO THE MASTER
STOOPED IN HIS PITY, AND GAVE HIM A PASS TO GO,
FOR THE SPACE OF A MOON, TO THE EARTH-WORLD,
TO MIX WITH THE MEN BELOW.

—ROBERT W. SERVICE

HOW DID THE ANGELS FALL?

There are many stories concerning the fall of the angels. And when you put them together, it all becomes about as clear as mud. The late author Taylor Caldwell wrote the novel *Dialogues with the Devil* in which Lucifer is given his "day in court." In it Lucifer appears as a powerful archangel, brother to Michael and Gabriel. In Lucifer's great love for God, he tempts humankind to its destruction, believing it is their just fate for turning away from the divine love of God.

In all the religions of the world, the sins of pride, disobedience and rebellion caused the fall of divine beings, just as they often cause sorrow and pain among humans today. Some say that Lucifer refused to acknowledge the divine within God's human creations and was cast out from heaven; others say he rebelled because he thought he could be "better" than God; yet others believe that Lucifer took on the task of tempter willingly. However the angels fell, the stories of their fall reflect man's attempt to personify evil and to come to grips with suffering.

WHERE IS THE FIRST MENTION OF FALLEN ANGELS?

The first mention of fallen angels is thought to be in the Bible. According to Gen. 6:1-5, some of the angels in heaven found the daughters of humans very beautiful and lusted after them. Against God's law, they took wives among the women.

The children of these unions were called "Nephilim." They were giants, much more powerful than the mothers that bore them, and, by all accounts, quite hungry! It is recorded that they soon ate everything around them.

This story in Genesis appears to be a fragment of another, longer story, probably borrowed from another culture. It is conceivable that these giants are none other than the ancient pagan gods, such as the gods of Olympus.

DID GOD MAKE BAD ANGELS?

According to the traditions, the fallen or bad angels decided by their own free will to follow Lucifer in his rebellion. God did not make them bad; he simply allowed them to choose good or evil.

119

In the same way, Christianity says that people have the choice of following good or evil. God will not interfere, because He has given people, like the angels, the gift of free will.

WHO IS SATAN?

In Hebrew, the word "satan" means "adversary." And in the Old Testament, Satan's role and function is to do God's will by being the adversary of man and woman.

We first encounter this angel of God in the story of Job. God asks Satan of his servant Job: "Is there not a more righteous and pious man on all the earth than he?" And Satan replies that if Job's life was made more difficult, he would soon find reason to turn against God. So God sends Satan to make Job's life miserable, and to test his faith.

Job suffers terrible events, but through it all comes to understand God's divine purpose. Satan is actually the inner adversary we deal with every day.

ARE LUCIFER AND SATAN THE SAME ANGEL?

Through the apocryphal writings, Satan emerges in the New Testament as the prince of evil and enemy of God, an explanation of the evil that exists in the world. Later Christians identified Lucifer as the angel who fell from heaven. Here is their interpretation of Isa. 14:12-15:

How you are fallen from heaven, O Day Star, son of Dawn! How you are cut down to the ground, you who laid the nations low! You said in your heart, "I will ascend to heaven: above the stars of God I will set my throne on high: I will sit on the mount of assembly in the far north: I will ascend above the heights of the clouds, I will make myself like the Most High". But you are brought down to Sheol (Hell), to the depths of the Pit.

Lucifer was considered a great archangel, closest to God, so it made sense that he would lead some of the heavenly host in rebellion. And as Satan was also identified as the prince of evil, the two names became intertwined.

CAN LUCIFER BE CONSIDERED GOOD?

Certainly in one tradition, it is Lucifer's great love for God and humankind that made him decide to take on the role of man's adversary. Lucifer's name means "light giver." He shows us the dark side of ourselves and humankind, so that we may understand and take joy in the good.

How can we experience joy, unless we know sorrow? One of my favorite poems is "Compensation", which I think says it all:

Who never wept knows laughter but a jest;
Who never failed, no victory has sought;
Who never suffered, never lived his best;
Who never doubted, never really thought;
Who never feared, real courage has not shown;
Who never faltered, lacks a real intent;
Whose soul was never troubled has not known
The sweetness and the peace of real content.

E. M. Brainard

It was William Blake who said of Lucifer, "Evil is only the deprivation of good, and when the soul emerges from this illusion of evil, Lucifer resumes his original status as one of God's great archangels."

ARE DEMONS FALLEN ANGELS?

The word demon comes from the Greek work "daemon." In the lore of that culture, daemons were thought to be benevolent spirits or guardian angels. The great Greek philosophers, Plato, Aristotle and Socrates, all maintained that they were very well acquainted with their daemons.

It is in Christian tradition that demons take on an evil connotation and are associated with the angels who fell with Satan. Jesus expelled demons from souls who were possessed. While in this day and age, we may brush aside the idea of demonic possession, the concept of evil is very real, whether it is a "bad angel" or our own negative thoughts.

IS THERE A HELL?

Certainly there are descriptions in Revelation concerning a pit of fire and brimstone. The Catholic Church teaches that hell is the last resting place of those judged to be unworthy, even after a stay in purgatory. The Greeks and Romans had their Hades as the resting place for the dead.

It's possible, however, that these depictions of hell are simply images humankind has conceived. Most of us have probably said at one time or another "That was sheer hell!" We experience hell as a state or time that seems to be terrible, something we wouldn't want anyone else to have to go through. Hell would appear to be more of a state of mind than a place of fire and brimstone.

WHO IS LILITH?

According to Jewish lore, Lilith was the most beautiful of all female demons and the bride of Satan. Legend has it that she was Adam's wife before Eve, but was deprived of this status when she refused to be subject to him, believing herself to be equal.

Four thousand years of folklore have produced a vast collection of stories on Lilith. Jewish women of the Middle Ages wore amulets to protect their newborn children from her. But men required help as well: Lilith and her female demons reportedly caused sleeping men to ejaculate in the night and collected the semen so they could bear children. All children born to Lilith were demons. The Zohar even claims that the Queen of Sheba was none other than the beautiful demoness. However, Lilith is mentioned only once as the "night hag" in the Bible (Isa. 34:14):

> *And wild beasts shall meet with hyenas,*
> *the satyr shall cry to his fellow;*
> *yea, there shall the night hag alight,*
> *and find for herself a resting place.*

The New Oxford Annotated Bible notes that the night hag is the demoness, Lilith.

HAS A FALLEN ANGEL EVER BEEN REDEEMED?

It was recorded that when the rebellion burst out in heaven, one third of the heavenly host fell. So many, in fact, that they supposedly fell for nine entire days! But Biblical scholars are of two minds concerning their redemption.

One school of thought believes that because the angels exercised their free will by deciding to join Satan, they must live forever with the consequences of that action. Others believe that a forgiving God would allow the angels back into the heavenly kingdom, if they repented.

WHAT ARE SOME OF THE NAMES OF ANGELS WHO HAVE FALLEN?

In the 15th century, Cardinal Bishop of Tusculum estimated that 133,306,668 angels fell with Satan. But it is a little more difficult to actually find the names of all of them. Besides the famous Satan and/or Lucifer, here's a list of names you might find familiar:

Asmodeus ("creature of judgement"—once of the seraphim)
Balaam (once of the dominions)
Beelzebub ("god of flies"—once of the cherubim)
Mammon ("greed for worldly riches")
Mephistopheles ("hater of light")
Raum (once of the thrones)
Uzziel ("strength of God"—once of the virtues)

NOTES

1. Stearn, *In Search of Taylor Caldwell*, 56.
2. Burnham, *A Book of Angels*, 150-151.
3. Bialow, *The Star*, March 15, 1994, 39.
4. Humann, *The Many Faces of Angels*, 12.
5. Burnham, *A Book of Angels*, 18-19.
6. Graham, *Angels, God's Secret Agents*, 27-28.
7. Roberts, *Daily Blessing*, 40-41.
8. Anderson, *Where Angels Walk*, 11.
9. *The Letters of Emily Dickinson*, letter no. 271.
10. Gibbs, *The New Age of Angels*, 56.
11. Smith, *In the Presence of Angels*, 18.
12. Atherley, *Someone to Watch Over Me*, 48.
13. Smith, *In the Presence of Angels*, 15.
14. Davidson, *A Dictionary of Angels*, 343.
15. ———, *A Dictionary of Angels*, 342.
16. Daniel, *Ask Your Angels*, 76-78.
17. Burnham, *Angel Letters*, 133-136.
18. Gibbs, *The New Age of Angels*, 61.
19. Davidson, *A Dictionary of Angels*, 343.
20. ———, *A Dictionary of Angels*, 351.
21. Ambelain, Robert, *La Kabbale Pratique*.
22. Davidson, *A Dictionary of Angels*, 338.
23. ———, *A Dictionary of Angels*, 240.
24. Burnham, *Angel Letters*, 65-70.

BIBLIOGRAPHY

Adler, Mortimer J. *The Angels and Us.* New York: MacMillan and Co., 1982.

Ambelain, Robert. *La Kabbale Pratique.* Paris: Editions Niclaus, 1951.

Anderson, Joan Wester. *Where Angels Walk.* New York: Ballantine, 1992.

"Angels," *Man Alive,* Toronto: Canadian Broadcasting Corporation, 1988.

Atherley, Ruth. "Someone to Watch Over Me," *MW,* August 1993: 48-51.

Atwater, P.M.H. "Perelandra, Cooperating Co-Creatively with Nature," *New Realities,* May/June 1988: 16.

Bialow, Jennifer. "Last Days and Final Words," *The Star,* March 15, 1994.

Bloom, William. *Devas, Fairies and Angels: A Modern Approach.* Glastonbury, England: Gothic Image Publications, 1986.

The Book of Common Praise, Being the Hymn Book of the Anglican Church of Canada. Oxford University Press. London: Amen House (revised 1938).

Burnham, Sophy. *Angel Letters.* New York: Ballantine Books, 1991.

———. *The Book of Angels.* New York: Ballantine Books, 1989.

Caldwell, Taylor. *Dialogues with the Devil.* New York: Fawcett Crest Books, 1967.

Daniel, Alma, Andrew Ramer and Timothy Wyllie. *Ask Your Angels*. New York: Ballantine Books, 1992.

Davidson, Gustav. *A Dictionary of Angels*. New York: Free Press, 1967.

Gibbs, Nancy. "Angels Among Us," *Time*, December 27, 1993: 55-65.

Goldman, Karen. *The Angel Book*. New York: Simon & Schuster, 1992.

The Gospel of the Essenes. Translated from the original Hebrew and Aramaic texts by Edmond Bordeaux Szekely. Saffron, England: The C.W. Daniel Co. Ltd., 1979.

Graham, Billy. *Angels, God's Secret Agents*. Waco, Texas: Word Books, 1976.

Hall, Manly P. *The Blessed Angels*. Los Angeles: The Philosophical Research Society, Inc., 1980.

Heywood, Thomas. *The Hierarchy of the Blessed Angels*. Norwood, N.J.: Walter J. Johnson, 1973.

Hilarion. *Other Kingdoms*. Toronto: Marcus Books, 1981.

Hodson, Geoffrey. *The Kingdom of the Gods*. Adyar, India: The Theosophical Publishing House, 1952.

Humann, Harvey. *The Many Faces of Angels*. Marina Del Rey, California: DeVorss & Company, 1986.

The Letters of Emily Dickinson. Cambridge, Massachusetts, 1958: letter no. 271.

The Lost Books of the Bible. New York: Crown Publishers, 1979 reprint of 1926 edition, first published in 1820.

MacGregor, Geddes. *Angels, Ministers of Grace*. New York: Paragon House, 1988.

MacLean, Dorothy. *To Hear the Angels Sing.* Issaquah, Washington: Morningtown Press, 1988.

Margolies, Morris B. *A Gathering of Angels: Angels in Jewish Life and Literature.* New York: Ballantine Books, 1994.

Moolenburgh, H.C. *A Handbook of Angels.* Saffron Walden, England: The C.W. Daniel Company Limited, 1984.

The New English Bible with Apocrypha. The Delegates of the Oxford University Press and the Syndics of the Cambridge University Press, 1970.

The New Oxford English Annotated Bible. Revised Standard Version, New York: Oxford University Press, 1973.

The Oxford Dictionary of Quotations. Third Edition, London: Oxford University Press, 1980.

Pagels, Elaine. *The Gnostic Gospels.* New York: Random House, 1979.

Roberts, Oral. *Daily Blessing.* Tarrytown, N.Y.: Fleming H. Revell Company, 1978.

Ronner, John. *Do You Have a Guardian Angel?* Indialantic, Florida: Mamre Press, 1985.

————. *Know Your Angels.* Murfreesboro, Tennessee: Mamre Press, 1993.

The Secret Teachings of Jesus, Four Gnostic Gospels. Translated by Marvin W. Meyer. New York: Random House, 1984.

Smith, Robert C. "In the Presence of Angels," *Venture Inward,* November/December 1993: 14-20.

Solara, ed. *Invoking Your Celestial Guardians.* Portal, Arizona: Star-Borne Unlimited, 1986.

Spunky, as told to Dan Campbell. "Have Wings, Will Travel," *Venture Inward*, November/December 1993: 48.

Stearn, Jess. *In Search of Taylor Caldwell*. New York: Bantam Books, 1981.

Swihart, Stephen D. *Angels in Heaven and Earth*. Plainfield, N.J.: Logos International, 1979.

Ward, Theodora. *Men and Angels*. New York: The Viking Press, 1969.

Woodward, Kenneth L. "Angels, Hark! America's Latest Search for Spiritual Meaning Has a Halo Effect," *Newsweek*, December 27, 1993: 52-56.

Zukav, Gary. *The Seat of the Soul*. New York: Simon and Schuster Inc., 1989.

ABOUT THE AUTHOR

Carolyn Trickey-Bapty grew up in Lachine, Québec, near the city of Montréal, where she enjoyed watching Les Canadiens play hockey and the Expos play baseball. She attended Carleton University in Ottawa, pursuing studies in history and religion, and it was there that she first wrote about angels. Recently, she was interviewed on the subject of angels for *Man Alive,* a Canadian Broadcasting Corporation weekly TV documentary.

After residing in Toronto and Edmonton for a number of years, Carolyn is currently living in Niagara Falls with her husband, Eric. Although she has spent most of her career in the financial industry, she is now looking forward to doing the two things she loves best—writing and working in her garden.

Carolyn would like to know what you think of angels. If you would like to share any questions, thoughts or experiences with her, please write:

Carolyn Trickey-Bapty
991 King Street West
P.O. Box 89068
Hamilton, Ontario L8S 4R5
CANADA